Women in Profile

Writers

Shaun Hunter

Crabtree Publishing Company

Dedication

This series is dedicated to every woman who has followed her dreams and to every young girl who hopes to do the same. While overcoming great odds and often oppression, the remarkable women in this series have triumphed in their fields. Their dedication, hard work, and excellence can serve as an inspiration to all—young and old, male and female. Women in Profile is both an acknowledgment of and a tribute to these great women.

Project Manager
Lauri Seidlitz
Crabtree Editor
Virginia Mainprize
Copy Editors
Krista McLuskey
Leslie Strudwick
Design and Layout
Warren Clark

Published by Crabtree Publishing Company

350 Fifth Avenue, Suite 3308
New York, NY
USA 10018

360 York Road, R.R. 4
Niagara-on-the-Lake
Ontario, Canada
L0S 1J0

Cataloging-in-Publication Data

Hunter, Shaun, 1961–
    Writers / Shaun Hunter.
        p. cm. — (Women in Profile)
    Includes bibliographical references and index.
    Summary: Introduces the lives and literary accomplishments of such women writers as Maya Angelou, Judy Blume, Astrid Lindgren, Jean Little, Lucy Maud Montgomery, and Beatrix Potter.
    ISBN 0-7787-0005-4. — ISBN 0-7787-0027-5 (pbk.)
    1. Women authors, North American—20th century—Biography—Juvenile literature. 2. Women and literature—North American—History—20th century—Juvenile literature. 3. North American literature—Women authors—History and criticism—Juvenile literature. 4. Women authors—Biography—Juvenile literature. [1. Women authors 2. Authors. 3. Women—Biography.]
I. Title. II. Series.
PS151.H86 1998
810.9'9287'0904—dc21
[b]
                97-53229
                CIP
                AC

Photograph Credits
Every reasonable effort has been made to trace ownership and to obtain permission to reprint copyright material. The publishers would be pleased to have any errors or omissions brought to their attention so that they may be corrected in subsequent printings. Archive Photos: pages 37, 38, 41; Courtesy of Judy Blume: pages 13, 14; Courtesy of Beverly Cleary: page 42; Corbis: cover, page 17; Corel Corporation: page 40; Frederick Warne & Co.: page 39 (Illustration from *The Tale of Peter Rabbit* by Beatrix Potter Copyright Frederick Warne & Co., 1987); Globe Photos, Inc.: pages 6 (Lisa Rose), 8 (S. Moskowitz), 11 (Henry McGee), 12, 16 (Michael Ferguson), 43 (Andrea Renault); Kvint Agency: pages 18 (Toni Sica), 23; Courtesy of Jean Little: pages 24, 25, 26, 27, 28, 29; Norman Lomax: page 45; Lordly & Dame, Inc.: page 9 (Steve Dunwell); L.M. Montgomery Collection, Special Collections, University of Guelph: pages 30, 32, 33, 34, 35 (*L.M. Montgomery, Emily,* and *Emily of New Moon* are trademarks of the Heirs of L.M. Montgomery Inc.); National Portrait Gallery, London: page 36; Photofest: pages 20, 22; Reuters/Corbis-Bettmann: page 10 (Gary Hershorn); Scholastic Inc.: page 44; Swedish Post stamps: page 21; UPI/Corbis-Bettmann: page 7 (Larry Rubenstein), 15 (John Neary).

Contents

More Women in Profile

Writers

When you look at the shelves of your local library or bookstore, you will probably see as many books by women writers as men. This has not always been the case. Until the twentieth century, women writers were few and far between. Most women never went to school. Reading and writing were the privilege of a small, mostly male group. A writing career was not an option for women. Until quite recently, a woman's primary work was raising children and looking after her family.

Over time, more and more women and men learned to read. And slowly, women began writing and being published. By the late eighteenth century, a small number of women had successful writing careers. Today, two hundred years later, there are many professional women writers.

However, women writers still face obstacles in their careers. As beginning writers, their work may be rejected many times by publishers. As mothers and wives, women must find time and space to write. As professional writers, they must work hard to make a living. Many writers are poorly paid for their work.

Each of the writers featured in this book has struggled with and overcome these obstacles and others. These women are just a few of the many talented and successful women writers of the twentieth century. Many of their works are books you may recognize from your own reading. The stories of these writers' lives reveal how and why they started writing and the challenges they met in their careers. Each of the six major profiles examines the writer's early years, her apprenticeship as a writer, and her accomplishments. The last section gives brief descriptions of several other writers about whom you may want to read on your own.

Perhaps the stories of these women and their careers as writers will inspire you to pursue your own dreams and develop your own talents.

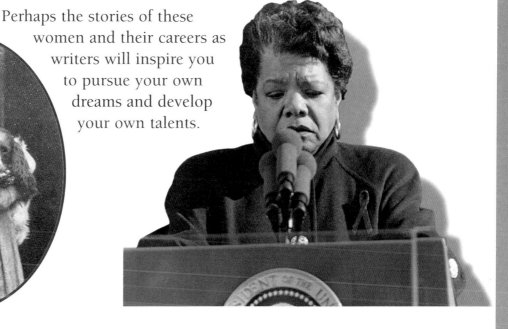

"I find the statement 'you can't' to be offensive to the human spirit. I think that we can be anything."

Maya Angelou

I Know Why the Caged Bird Sings

Early Years

Marguerite Johnson was born in St. Louis, Missouri. Her younger brother, Bailey, called her "mya sister." Soon, Marguerite became known as Maya. When she was three years old, her parents decided to divorce. Maya and Bailey were sent to Stamps, Arkansas, to live with their grandmother. Still toddlers, the children traveled alone by train to Stamps. On their wrists, they wore tags with their names and destination.

Maya grew up in an African-American neighborhood in Stamps. During a visit to her mother in St. Louis, Maya was sexually assaulted by her mother's boyfriend. Maya was just seven years old. When she told her family about the incident, the boyfriend was killed. Convinced that her voice could kill, Maya stopped talking to everyone except her brother. Her silence lasted five years.

Back in Stamps, Maya worked hard at school. She read as much as she could, including African-American writers such as W.E.B. DuBois, Langston Hughes, and Paul Laurence.

BACKGROUNDER

Segregation

In 1865, after the American Civil War, slavery was **abolished** in the United States. However, **racial prejudice** continued in the form of **segregation**. Mainly in the American South, African Americans and white Americans were treated as unequal groups. African Americans had to attend separate schools and colleges, travel in separate sections on buses and trains, and use separate public facilities.

Maya often writes about her own childhood experiences.

Developing Skills

W hen she was thirteen, a friend of her grandmother helped Maya regain her voice. Maya was allowed to borrow books from this woman's library, but only if she would read them out loud. About that time, Maya started to write poetry. When she was fourteen, Maya moved to San Francisco to live with her mother. She won a dance and drama scholarship and decided to become a professional dancer. At sixteen, she became pregnant. Maya kept her pregnancy a secret and finished high school.

Maya's early experience as an entertainer helped her win a Grammy Award in 1994 for best spoken word album for "On the Pulse of Morning."

Maya then started a series of odd jobs, including waitressing, exotic dancing, and operating a cable car. Maya was the first African-American woman to work as a cable car conductor.

She was discovered as a talented blues and calypso singer at the famous Purple Onion nightclub in San Francisco. It was at the Purple Onion that Maya adopted the name Angelou. She took the name from her first husband, Tosh Angelos. Her success as an entertainer took her through Europe, Africa, and the United States.

In her early thirties, Maya and her son moved to New York City. She joined the Harlem Writers Guild, a group of African-American authors who met to discuss their work. Here, Maya received encouragement for her poems and plays. She also began to think about writing her own life story.

In New York, Maya became inspired by Martin Luther King, Jr. and the **civil rights** movement. King wanted to end racism in the United States. Maya found a job in the northern office of King's Southern Christian Leadership Conference. She also produced the play *Cabaret for Freedom* to raise money to fight prejudice.

In 1961, Maya moved to Egypt with her second husband, a freedom fighter from South Africa. After their marriage ended, she moved to Ghana, a country in West Africa. During these years, Maya was writing. She worked as a journalist, **editor**, and lecturer.

"*We were Black Americans living in West Africa, where for the first time in our lives the color of our skin was accepted as correct and normal.*"

BACKGROUNDER

The Civil Rights Movement

The Southern Christian Leadership Conference (S.C.L.C.) was founded in 1957 to work for equal rights for African Americans. Led by Martin Luther King, Jr., the S.C.L.C. did not believe in using violence to reach its goals. In the early 1960s, it led the campaign for desegregating schools, restaurants, hotels, and department stores in Birmingham, Alabama. In 1963, it organized a huge protest march in Washington, D.C. There, Dr. King delivered his famous "I Have a Dream" speech. This speech inspired thousands of people to end segregation.

BACKGROUNDER

"On the Pulse of Morning"

On a sunny January day in 1993, Maya stood to read her poem "On the Pulse of Morning" at the **inauguration** of President Bill Clinton. Maya's poem called to Americans of all backgrounds to remember their history and be hopeful for the future. President Clinton chose Maya to deliver the poem for several reasons. Both he and Maya had grown up in Arkansas, in towns not far apart. Most important, Maya had triumphed over her difficult childhood. Clinton hoped that Maya's poem would inspire all Americans to overcome their difficulties as individuals and as a society.

Maya's poem "On the Pulse of Morning" is about people who have tried to find a new life in America.

Accomplishments

Maya returned to the United States in the 1960s. She wrote and published her poetry. She also started working in film and television, writing scripts, producing, and acting. In 1970, she published *I Know Why the Caged Bird Sings*. It was the first in a series of books about her life. It quickly became a bestseller.

Between 1970 and 1986, Maya published five books about her life. Maya's **autobiographies** are about more than just one woman's experience. In talking about her writing, Maya has said, "I use the first person singular, [but] I'm talking about the third person plural all the time; what it's like to be a human being." Maya writes about experiences that many other men and women share. Maya's books are often used in courses on African-American and women's studies.

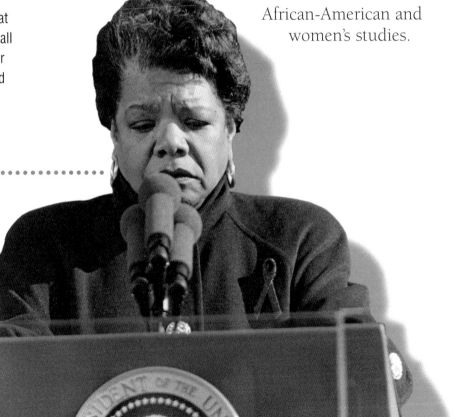

Throughout her career, Maya has been honored for her achievements as a fine writer and a model citizen. In 1975, United States President Gerald Ford appointed her to the American Revolution Bicentennial Advisory Council. Later that year, United States President Jimmy Carter named her to a national committee for the observance of International Women's Year. In 1993, she read a poem at the inauguration of United States President Bill Clinton. Maya was the first African American and first woman to speak at an American presidential inauguration.

Since 1982, Maya has served as a professor in American Studies at Wake Forest University in North Carolina. In 1982, Maya was given a lifetime appointment to the American studies department at Wake Forest University.

She continues to write poetry and tell stories about her own life. Maya's work is very personal. She has compared writing to "dragging my pencil across the old scars to sharpen it."

Quick Notes

- Maya speaks six languages: English, French, Spanish, Italian, Arabic, and Fanti.

- In 1972, Maya was the first African-American woman to have a screenplay produced. The film *Georgia, Georgia* was nominated for the Pulitzer Prize.

- Maya wrote the screenplay and music for the 1979 film adaptation of her book *I Know Why the Caged Bird Sings*.

- Maya starred in the television mini-series *Roots*, Alex Haley's tale of an African-American family. Maya played Kunta Kinte's grandmother.

"All my work, my life, everything is about survival. All my work is meant to say, 'You may encounter many defeats, but you must not be defeated.'"

Maya at a 1997 book signing for Even the Stars Look Lonesome.

KEY EVENTS

1961 Graduates from New York University with a degree in elementary education

1967-68 Takes a course on writing for children and teenagers at New York University

1970 Publishes *Are You There God? It's Me, Margaret*

1975 Divorces John Blume after sixteen years of marriage

1978 Publishes first novel for adults, *Wifey*

1981 Establishes the Kids' Fund to assist non-profit organizations that help young people

1983 Receives the Eleanor Roosevelt Humanitarian Award

1996 Receives the Margaret Edwards Award

1998 Publishes *Summer Sisters*

"My responsibility to be honest with my readers is my strongest motivation. I am offended by dishonest books. I hate the idea that you should always protect children. They live in the same world we do."

Judy Blume

Are You There God? It's Me, Margaret

Early Years

Judy Sussman grew up in Elizabeth, New Jersey. She and her family lived in a house filled with books. An imaginative child, Judy made up her own stories. She also enjoyed dance and drama. One summer, she put on a play starring herself and her friends. Judy was a good student. She graduated from high school with high honors and then enrolled at New York University. She planned to be an elementary school teacher.

Judy also planned to get married and have a family. During university, she met and married John Blume. By the time she graduated, she was expecting her first child. Her teaching career went on hold. She recalls, "My mother prepared me for marriage and motherhood, but it wasn't enough. I needed something of my own." She became frustrated with her life as a housewife.

BACKGROUNDER

Feminism in the 1960s

In the 1960s, many women in North America were talking about the status of women. They called for changes to society to give women the same opportunities as men. In 1963, Betty Friedan wrote *The Feminine Mystique*. Friedan said that women had few choices aside from being housewives and mothers. She wrote that women needed more options for their lives. This interest in women's rights was called the second wave of **feminism** in North America. The first wave took place in the early part of the twentieth century when women worked to win the right to vote.

Judy started taking dance lessons when she was three. As an adult she has taken tap dancing.

Developing Skills

Judy started looking for ways to use her talent. She wrote songs and designed colorful felt banners for children. Neither project was a success.

Then Judy read about a night course at New York University on writing for children and teenagers. She enrolled immediately. Reading books to her young son and daughter made Judy want to write children's books. She had said to herself, "I could do this." The course soon became the highlight of her life. Judy wrote constantly and received praise from her teacher. She learned about the business of writing and started sending her stories to magazines and book publishers.

At first, Judy received many rejections from publishers. The rejections were disappointing. Judy remembers, however, that during these early years she "began to feel like a professional writer." Eventually, magazines began to publish some of her stories. A publisher bought one of her picture books and her first novel, *Iggie's House*.

Judy's first stories imitated the books she liked reading to her children. After a while, she decided to try a new kind of writing. She wanted "to try to write the kinds of books I wished I'd had to read when I was young. Books about real life."

Judy wrote **Iggie's House** *while taking a night class in writing. She wrote one chapter a week.*

Judy went to work on what was to become one of her most successful books, *Are You There God? It's Me, Margaret.* This novel tells the story of eleven-year-old Margaret Simon and her experience of growing up. The book deals with subjects rarely found in children's literature. Some critics did not think the book was suitable for children. When the paperback version was published in 1972, most young readers thought otherwise. They made *Are You There God? It's Me, Margaret* a bestseller.

Soon, Judy was writing books about many **controversial** topics. Her characters deal with **puberty**, sexuality, peer cruelty, shoplifting, premarital sex, and other issues. Judy's story ideas come from her vivid imagination, her own experiences, and those she hears about from family and friends. She remembers clearly the details of her own childhood.

Judy receives hundreds of letters each week from readers asking her for advice.

"Margaret came right out of my own sixth grade life, except for the family situation. Her feelings, her actions, her friends, her concerns—they were all the things we were interested in in the sixth grade."

Censorship

Censorship is control over books, films, art, and ideas. Some people fear that certain ideas will harm individuals or society and they try to stop them. Censorship sometimes happens in schools. Some people are concerned about the information and ideas available to children. Some groups object to material containing coarse language and mature subject matter. In Texas, the state's Textbook Commission must approve all books used in public schools. Other groups, such as the American Library Association, oppose censorship and promote children's freedom to read.

Accomplishments

After the success of *Are You There God? It's Me, Margaret* in 1970, Judy earned enough money to feel she could support herself. She also had confidence in herself as a writer. Her success came at some personal cost. In 1975, Judy's sixteen-year marriage to John Blume ended. She then had a very brief second marriage and has been married to her third husband, George Cooke, since 1980.

Judy has said, "I owe my career to my readers." Many of her books have been bestsellers. In 1983, paperback sales of her books reached twenty-seven million copies. Today, world sales have reached sixty-five million. Young readers love Judy's books. However, her honest books have sparked controversy among some adults. A few of her books have been banned from school libraries.

Her 1975 book for young adults, *Forever*, met with disapproval from some librarians and other people. *Forever* is the story of two high school students who fall in love and eventually have sexual intercourse. Their story ends positively. Even so, Judy's paperback publisher turned the book down. The book was first published as an adult novel.

Judy at the launch of a new book in 1994.

But Judy stands by her book. She knows that many twelve- and thirteen-year-olds read *Forever*. She hopes she is helping young people make responsible decisions.

Judy has a strong connection with her readers. She receives thousands of letters a year from young people who value her truthful writing about their lives and concerns. Judy champions the rights of young people. In 1981, she established the Kids' Fund with royalties from one of her writing projects. The Kids' Fund provides up to $40,000 a year to organizations that help young people. In 1986, she published *Letters to Judy: What Your Kids Wish They Could Tell You*, which was also a Kids' Fund Project.

In 1996, the American Library Association awarded Judy the Margaret Edwards Award for contributing a lasting body of work. They specifically mentioned the book Forever *when giving the award.*

Quick Notes

- Judy has written three novels for adults, *Wifey* (1978) and *Smart Women* (1984). Her third, *Summer Sisters,* was published in 1998.

- Judy worked with her son, Larry, to produce the 1989 film of her book *Otherwise Known as Sheila the Great.*

- Judy's book *Starring Sally J. Freedman as Herself* (1977) is part **autobiography**. The book tells the story of a ten-year-old Jewish-American girl growing up in the 1940s.

- *Fudge,* a television series based on the characters in *Tales of a Fourth Grade Nothing,* has been on television for several seasons.

"I felt ... that I had to write the most honest books I could.... It never occurred to me, at the time, that what I was writing about was controversial."

"When I write, I lie in bed … and I have the feeling that nothing outside exists—I'm just on my bed in my little room, and I can go and meet the people I want to."

Astrid Lindgren

Pippi Longstocking

Early Years

A strid Ericsson grew up in the Swedish countryside near the town of Vimmerby. Her family farmed the same land that her grandparents and her great-grandparents had farmed before them. The four Ericsson children were free to roam and play. As a young girl, Astrid loved stories. Her father often told stories to his children about his own childhood.

Once she started school, Astrid became an eager reader. When she put her younger sister to bed, Astrid would sing whatever book she was reading until her sister fell asleep. In the summer, she and her **siblings** acted out stories. One year, they acted out scenes from one of their favorite books, *Anne of Green Gables*. Astrid's school friends were sure she would be a great writer one day. But Astrid disagreed. "That scared me so much that I made a firm decision—never to write a book!" She did not change her mind until she was forty-two years old.

BACKGROUNDER

Sweden

Sweden is the largest country in Scandinavia. Scandinavia is made up of five countries in northwestern Europe: Sweden, Denmark, Norway, Finland, and Iceland. The capital city of Sweden, Stockholm, has a population of 700,000 people. Stockholm is on the coast of the Baltic Sea. Swedish winters are long and harsh with very few hours of daylight. Summer days are long, with the sun shining twenty-four hours a day in parts of northern Sweden.

The Origins of Pippi Longstocking

When Astrid's seven-year-old daughter, Karin, became ill with pneumonia, Astrid told her stories each night. Eventually, she ran out of ideas for new stories. One night, Karin asked her mother to tell her about Pippi Longstocking. Astrid recalls, "I didn't ask who Pippi Longstocking was, I just started telling a story about her. And because she had such a funny name, she turned out to be a funny little girl." After Karin got better, Astrid broke her ankle. While she was bedridden, she decided to write down the Pippi stories. She wanted to give them to Karin as a birthday gift. When she was finished, she sent the stories to a publisher. They were rejected. Undiscouraged, Astrid entered another story in a publisher's contest and won second prize. The next year, she sent the Pippi Longstocking story to the same contest. Pippi was awarded first prize and was soon published as a book.

One of Pippi's more unusual qualities is her enormous strength.

Developing Skills

When she was nineteen, Astrid left the farm. She moved to the city of Stockholm. There, she attended secretarial school and found work. At one of her jobs, she met Sture Lindgren. They married and raised two children.

In the early years of her marriage, Astrid started to write a diary. She recorded her observations of events in Europe that would eventually lead to World War II. The diary became a regular part of her life. Astrid often entertained her young children with stories she made up. Out of these stories the character Pippi Longstocking was born. Astrid decided to write down Pippi's story.

Pippi Longstocking met with mixed reviews. Some critics did not approve of this unusual nine-year-old girl. Pippi lives alone in a falling-down house with a monkey and a horse. Rather than going to school, she has adventures with other children. Pippi is also kind, independent, and loyal to her friends. Children immediately loved Pippi. The book sold well and was eventually translated into fifty languages around the world.

With the success of *Pippi Longstocking*, Astrid launched her career as a writer of books for children. She also began to work as an **editor** of children's books. In the mornings, Astrid wrote her own stories. She often wrote in bed, the same way she wrote *Pippi Longstocking*. She used the shorthand she learned as a young woman in secretarial school.

In the afternoons, she worked at her publishing company, Rabén and Sjögren. She selected American children's books for translation into Swedish. Over the years, the company became one of the biggest children's book publishers in Sweden. Astrid played an important role in the company's success, not only as an editor, but also as one of the company's most successful authors.

"Everything I write has really taken its hue from my own experience, perhaps not directly, but indirectly, like some kind of breeding ground from which the books grow."

In 1996, Sweden issued a postage stamp in Astrid's honor.

Accomplishments

For thirty years, Astrid wrote one book a year. Her Pippi books are perhaps the most well known. However, Astrid created books about many other characters, such as Mischievous Meg, Bill Bergson, Emil, and the children of Noisy Village. Astrid also wrote fairy tales, picture books, plays, film scripts, and career and travel books.

Astrid has become the most translated of all Swedish writers. The character of Pippi Longstocking has appeared in comic strips, picture books, a play, a television series, and movies. By 1996, more than one million copies of *Pippi Longstocking* had been sold in Sweden. This is a remarkable success, since Sweden's population is just over eight million. Astrid's work as a writer and editor helped her to support her family during her husband's illness and after his death in 1952.

From the 1988 film, **The New Adventures of Pippi Longstocking.**

With the popularity of her books, Astrid Lindgren became a well-known public figure in Sweden. When she was in her seventies, she began writing about issues of concern to her. In 1976, in a satiric story for adults that she wrote for a Swedish newspaper, she drew attention to the high income tax rate. That year, the ruling party lost an election after forty years in power. The new government lowered taxes. Some people credit Astrid with the government's downfall.

Astrid also drew attention to the poor treatment of farm animals in Sweden. She protested farming methods that kept pigs and chickens in cages that were so small that the animals could not move. Her letters to the editor often took the form of fairy tales for adults. In 1987, the government introduced a new animal protection law. This law became known as the Lindgren Law.

BACKGROUNDER

Satire

Since ancient times, writers and artists have used satire to expose and criticize aspects of their society. Subjects of satires through the ages have included foolishness, vanity, **hypocrisy**, **bigotry**, and the abuse of power. Targets can be governments, groups, or individuals. Sometimes satire is gently critical. Other times it can be biting. Many satirists want their work to cause change in society.

"If I've succeeded in brightening up just one gloomy childhood, I'm satisfied."

" I write books about children and the thorny problems that beset them ... because I remember how it was."

Jean Little

Mine for Keeps

Early Years

Jean Little spent the first seven years of her life in Taiwan. Both her parents were Canadian medical doctors working as **missionaries**. Jean was born with scars that covered the pupils of her eyes. As she grew, her vision slowly improved. But almost everything Jean saw was blurry. Her parents wanted to make sure that their daughter did not see herself as disabled. Along with her two brothers and sister, Jean had a busy and active childhood.

As a young girl, Jean loved listening to stories. She could hardly wait to learn how to read. Her mother ordered special books from Canada with large print. With a great deal of hard work, Jean learned how to read. Jean's parents decided to move their young family back to Canada where Jean could attend a special class in the same school as her brothers and sister.

BACKGROUNDER

Raising Children with Disabilities

Jean's parents were determined not to treat their daughter differently because of her poor eyesight. Even though Jean often stumbled and fell, her parents encouraged her to play with the other children in the mission. Jean even climbed trees with her friends. Jean did not know she was different from other children until she was five. When she was older, children called her "cross-eyed," but by then Jean took comfort in reading and her talent for writing.

(far left) Jean with her mother and dog Zephyr. (this page) Jean at age six with her brother Hugh at Repulse Bay, Hong Kong.

Developing Skills

At school, Jean was an outsider. She had few friends and was often teased by the other children. Jean coped with her loneliness. She became very close to her family. She also found strength in books and her imagination. Jean was a good storyteller. She often got herself out of scrapes at school by telling a story. In fifth grade, she began writing her own stories. Soon, she began writing poetry. Jean's father supported his daughter's writing. He was an amateur writer himself. He helped publish thirty of her poems and sold the small book to friends and family. He told Jean, "This is only your first book."

Jean decided to study literature at university. Her teachers at the University of Toronto did not think she could handle all the reading she would have to do. She convinced them to let her try. She hired readers at first but found this way of learning too slow. Her father helped her with research. However, during her second year, he had a heart attack and died. Jean continued with her studies alone. She did her own reading and relied on her listening skills and her memory. Four years after starting university, she graduated first in her class.

"If I wanted to read what was written on the board [at school] I would have to stand up so that my face was only inches away from the writing. Then I would have to walk back and forth, following the words not only with my eyes but with my entire body."

Jean at age seventeen.

After graduation, Jean took courses on teaching children with disabilities. She returned to her hometown, Guelph, Ontario, to help organize a school for children with muscular difficulties. The idea of writing a novel, however, was always in Jean's mind. At university, she had written a short novel and submitted it to a publisher. The **manuscript** was returned, but the publisher said she had talent as a writer.

When she was twenty-eight, Jean took a year off teaching to give novel-writing a second try. She wrote the story of a girl living with cerebral palsy, a disability that affects the muscles. In 1961, *Mine for Keeps* won the award for the year's best Canadian children's book.

The success of *Mine for Keeps* allowed Jean to quit her teaching job. She decided to become a full-time writer. However, her sight was getting worse. She had several unsuccessful operations to improve it. Finally, her doctors decided to remove her left eye.

BACKGROUNDER

Children with Disabilities in Literature

When Jean was teaching children with disabilities, she began looking for better stories to read to them. Jean was frustrated with books about people with disabilities. They always seemed to end with a wonderful cure or death. Jean believed that all children, including children with disabilities, have a need to find themselves represented in fiction. With her first novel, *Mine for Keeps*, Jean provided children with disabilities an opportunity to read about children like themselves.

During her years as a teacher, Jean studied education at the University of Utah in the summer. One year, she took a course in creative writing taught by an award-winning children's author. This course inspired Jean to consider a career in writing.

Meeting Rosemary Sutcliffe

Jean had always admired the work of the British writer Rosemary Sutcliffe. Rosemary had been writing historical fiction for young people for many years. Jean had read Rosemary's novel *Warrior Scarlet* to her students. She and her students found the story of the young hero disabled in battle believable and compelling. During her own surgeries, Jean had also found strength and inspiration in Rosemary's books. She sent copies of her first two books to Rosemary and received warm praise in return. Jean had no idea that Rosemary had been disabled since childhood by a form of juvenile arthritis. In 1965, during a European trip, Jean arranged to meet Rosemary. The two writers formed a lasting friendship.

Jean (second from left) and her seeing eye dog Zephyr, with their class at the Seeing Eye School.

Accomplishments

Despite losing one eye, Jean continued to write. Through the 1960s and 1970s, she wrote eleven books for young readers. Jean has written about children with disabilities such as cerebral palsy and blindness. But many of her books are about able-bodied children coping with death, loneliness, family, and friendship.

She traveled throughout North America to give readings. Eventually, she began having problems with her right eye. She could no longer live or travel alone. She could not type. Jean became depressed and angry.

Jean did not want to give up writing. She developed a way to write using two tape recorders and a typist. But writing was slow and frustrating. In 1984, she had finished *Mama's Going to Buy You a Mockingbird*. This book had taken seven years to write.

Two things happened to change Jean's life. First, she was accepted by the Seeing Eye School, the oldest guide dog school in North America. At age fifty, she became a student again. After weeks of difficult training, she received her first seeing eye dog, Zephyr.

Second, Jean heard about a new development in computer technology. A blind man living close to Jean had developed software that could translate the human voice into written form. With the help of grants and donations, Jean got her own talking computer. She calls her computer SAM (for synthesized audio microcomputer). With Zephyr and SAM, Jean had the independence she needed to continue her writing.

Quick Notes

- In her 1995 book, *His Banner over Me,* Jean tells the story of her mother. Flora Little was one of the first female doctors in Canada.

- Jean has written two **autobiographies**, *Little by Little: A Writer's Education* (1987) and *Stars Come Out Within* (1990).

Jean at age fifty-nine with her seeing eye dog Ritz.

"I wanted to be a writer, but I had been told over and over again that you could not make a living as a writer. You had to get a real job and write in your spare time."

Developing Skills

Storytelling came naturally to Maud. She listened to the adults in her community tell stories about the past. She also listened to gossip, as the adults told stories about one another. At an early age, Maud started telling her own stories and writing poetry. She wrote long letters to her father who lived on the western prairies. She began writing a journal at age nine. Maud continued her journal until she died at age sixty-eight.

When she was sixteen, Maud spent a year with her father and his new family in the west. During her stay, she sent some of her poems to magazines. She soon learned that one of her poems had been published in a Prince Edward Island magazine, the *Charlottetown Patriot*. Maud returned to her grandparents' home to finish high school. Later, she graduated from teachers' college and began to teach on the island. She also continued to write. She woke up early each morning and wrote for an hour before going to work.

Maud at age fourteen.

She left her teaching career for a year to study English literature in Halifax, Nova Scotia. At that time, she started selling her stories to magazines. Popular women's magazines were interested in publishing romantic stories. Maud received good fees for her **sentimental** stories. In her late twenties, she was a successful writer earning about $500 a year. However, Maud did not think her magazine stories were serious writing. She preferred writing poetry.

For most of her twenties and thirties, Maud looked after her grandmother in Cavendish. She spent several months as a copy **editor** and writer at the Halifax *Daily Echo*. But for the most part, Maud ran her grandmother's household. She squeezed in her writing when she could. It was an unhappy period in Maud's life. During these years, Maud had started writing a story about an orphan girl named Anne Shirley. The **manuscript** was rejected five times, so Maud put it away in a box. Several years later, she pulled it out and reworked the story. This time, a publisher accepted *Anne of Green Gables* and immediately asked Maud to write a **sequel**.

After Maud's grandmother died, she was free to begin a new chapter in her life. Several years before, she had secretly become engaged to Ewan Macdonald. Ewan was a **Presbyterian** minister in Cavendish. After she and Ewan were married, they moved to a small town in Ontario. Maud then juggled three careers: minister's wife, mother of two children, and famous writer.

BACKGROUNDER

The Popularity of *Anne of Green Gables*

Millions of people throughout the world have enjoyed the adventures of Anne Shirley. The success of the Anne books has been remarkable. In the first five years, *Anne of Green Gables* was reprinted thirty-two times. It is still an international bestseller. Anne's story has been made into two movies, two television serials, and a musical. Maud never believed Anne's story would be so successful. Eventually, she grew tired of Anne. After the sixth book, *Anne of Ingleside*, Maud remarked, "I have gone completely 'stale' on Anne and must get a new heroine. Six books are enough to write about any girl." Altogether, Maud wrote eight books about the life of Anne Shirley.

Maud in 1908, around the time Anne of Green Gables *was published. When it was first published,* Anne of Green Gables *was sold as a book for adults.*

Quick Notes

- Maud's books introduced Prince Edward Island to the world. In 1936, the Canadian government decided to make the area around Maud's home in Cavendish a national park.

- Maud did not think her Anne books were her best. Her favorite was *The Story Girl* which she considered a more literary book.

- In 1920, Maud wrote about a new character, Emily Starr. Like Anne, Emily was an orphan. But like Maud, Emily was a writer who felt set apart from her world. Emily has since inspired many successful writers early in their careers.

Maud at age forty-five.

"*Everything [in Prince Edward Island] was invested with a kind of fairy grace charm, emanating from my own fancy.*"

Accomplishments

In Ontario, Maud was busy with her young family and helping her husband with his church duties. But she continued to write two hours each day. She worked on her novels, stories, articles, memoirs, and poems. She also wrote long letters to friends and family. She recorded her thoughts and observations in her journal. Maud was a popular speaker and often traveled to give readings.

She earned a lot of money from her writing. Two years after she published *Anne of Green Gables*, Maud was receiving over $7,000 a year in royalties. The average yearly income for working women in those days was less than $300. Unlike most women at the time, she kept her earnings separate from her husband's, and she managed her own business affairs.

Maud often returned to Prince Edward Island for long vacations. The island remained the setting and inspiration for much of her writing. The stories Maud told in her books, however, did not echo her own life as an adult. Maud's characters face life with good humor and courage. Their stories are often funny, and sometimes sentimental.

Maud herself had a more gloomy outlook and often felt helpless. She did not enjoy many of her duties as a minister's wife. She once wrote in her journal, "Those whom the gods wish to destroy they make ministers' wives." Maud's own religious views were not always the same as those of her husband and their church. Through the years, Maud's husband often suffered from depression. Maud felt helpless because she could not help him.

World War I also weighed heavily on Maud. Many men from her small town were killed. Just as the war ended, her cousin and close friend died of the influenza epidemic. When Maud was sixty-three, she also suffered a period of depression. She recorded her deepest feelings in her journals. Much of her journals was published in the 1980s. They tell us a lot about Maud and about women's lives at the time.

BACKGROUNDER

World War I

World War I was known as the Great War. It was fought mainly in Europe between 1914 and 1918. People had never before seen a war of this type. The war killed ten million people and wounded another twenty million. Immediately following the war, another twenty million people died from the influenza epidemic.

Maud at age sixty-one. When Maud died seven years later, she was buried in Cavendish cemetery on Prince Edward Island.

"I have never quite understood the secret of Peter's perennial charm. Perhaps it is because he and his friends keep on their way, busily absorbed in their own doings. They were always independent."

Beatrix Potter

The Tale of Peter Rabbit

Early Years

Beatrix Potter had an unusual childhood in London, England. She grew up in a wealthy neighborhood with her younger brother and her parents. Beatrix spent much of her childhood by herself or with her brother. She was taught by governesses who came to the house. Afraid of germs, her mother would not allow her daughter to play with other children.

As a young child, Beatrix was fascinated with animals, insects, and plants. She and her brother often brought home animals—dead or alive—to study and draw. Beatrix also had pets, including two rabbits and a hedgehog. Some of these animals would one day become the models for her famous animal characters.

BACKGROUNDER

The Secret Journal

No one knew about Beatrix's secret journal until nine years after she died. In 1952, a cousin found a bundle of papers in a drawer in the attic of Beatrix's farmhouse. The pages were written in a code language Beatrix had invented herself. It took four years to crack the code and make sense of the journal. Although secret, the journal did not contain any secret information. Instead, Beatrix had recorded details about her daily life from about age fourteen to thirty-one. The journal ended just before her most creative period, when she began writing books for children.

From an early age, Beatrix relied upon herself and her pets for amusement.

Developing Skills

Beatrix's father encouraged his daughter's talents. Together, they visited the Natural History Museum so that Beatrix could sketch. The Potter family enjoyed long summer holidays in the countryside. There, Beatrix found many subjects to draw.

Beatrix started writing about natural science. In about 1888, she began a serious study of **fungi**. She drew and painted samples of these small organisms. Impressed with her careful work, her uncle introduced Beatrix to some scientists in London. Unfortunately, they would not take the work of this young woman seriously.

Beatrix loved spending time in the country.

Beatrix decided that she could not succeed as a woman scientist. She turned her attention back to her earlier love, drawing her pet rabbits and other small creatures. She spent hours at London's museums sketching. In 1890, Beatrix sold some of her drawings of rabbits to be used on Christmas cards. She began to think about turning some of her animal stories into books.

Beatrix usually shared her drawings only with close friends and family. She was still in touch with one of her former governesses, Annie Carter. Annie had married and had children of her own. When Annie's five-year-old son, Noël, became ill, Beatrix wrote him a letter illustrated with small pen-and-ink drawings. Many letters followed to Annie's children, including stories about a squirrel named Nutkin. The stories Beatrix told in these letters contained ideas for the books she was to write several years later.

Seven years after Beatrix had written to Noël, she asked to borrow back her letters. She had decided to publish her text and sketches. She sent the **manuscript** to six different publishers. Six letters of rejection came back. Beatrix did not give up. She decided to use her savings to publish the book herself. The first run of 250 copies was so popular that she had another 200 copies printed. A friend of the Potter family sent the book to the Frederick Warne publishing company. Warne decided to publish the book in 1902. Within one year, almost fifty-thousand copies of *The Tale of Peter Rabbit* had been printed. Since then, the book has been translated into many languages.

BACKGROUNDER

The Tale of Peter Rabbit

"'Now my dears,' said old Mrs. Rabbit one morning, 'you may go into the fields or down the lane, but don't go into Mr. McGregor's garden: your Father had an accident there; he was put in a pie by Mrs. McGregor.'" Mrs. Rabbit's warning to her children is ignored by Peter Rabbit in this famous tale of his adventures in Mr. McGregor's garden. Peter escapes, but he leaves his jacket and shoes behind. His clothing becomes a scarecrow for Mr. McGregor, and Peter is sent to bed without any dinner.

Like this good tale, all of Beatrix's stories use humor. Readers are drawn into stories about a group of woodland characters that include Squirrel Nutkin, Mr. Jeremy Fisher, Jemima Puddle-duck, and Mrs. Tittlemouse.

Beatrix's sketch from The Tale of Peter Rabbit.

Quick Notes

- As children, Beatrix and her brother created their own printing press. They made ink from soot and coal oil.

- When she was thirty-nine, Beatrix became secretly engaged to Norman Warne, the son of her publisher, Frederick Warne. Her parents did not approve and tried to prevent the marriage. The same year, Norman died suddenly.

- *The Journal of Beatrix Potter* was published in 1966, one hundred years after her birth. It contained the stories of her life that Beatrix wrote down in her secret journal.

The Lake District in England, where Beatrix had her farm, is well known for its beautiful scenery.

Accomplishments

For ten years after the success of *The Tale of Peter Rabbit*, Beatrix published two books a year. She was very fussy about the details of her books. They had to be a certain size, bound in a special way, and contain high-quality illustrations. She insisted that the books be small enough for a child to hold them easily. Beatrix always tested her stories in draft form, sending them to the children she knew.

During her writing career, Beatrix published twenty-three books for children. The success of her books allowed Beatrix to gain independence from her parents. In 1905, she bought her own property, Hill Top Farm, in the Lake District in northwest England. Beatrix was happy being a country farmer. She loved being far away from the formal society of London. The countryside inspired her art. Many of the landscapes, animals, and people in her books could be found in and around Hill Top Farm.

Beatrix soon bought a second property in the same area, Castle Cottage Farm. At that time, she met William Heelis, a local lawyer who gave her real estate advice. She and William became close friends. In 1913, they married. Beatrix was forty-seven years old. After her marriage, Beatrix wrote less and less. She devoted herself to her farms and her sheep. Beatrix's farms were largely responsible for preserving a rare kind of English sheep, the Herdwick breed.

Beatrix worked to save the Lake District's landscapes. She raised money for the National Trust and donated her land to the Trust. Today, visitors can wander through Hill Top Farm. The farmhouse still contains Beatrix's furniture, china, and pictures. Her drawings are on display in Hawkshead village in a building where William Heelis once worked.

BACKGROUNDER

The National Trust

In England in the late 1890s, the National Trust for Places of Historic Interest or Natural Beauty was formed. Beatrix Potter and others wanted to save England's special places. The number of tourists in the countryside was growing. Roads for their cars and buildings to house and feed visitors were already changing the Lake District and other areas. Beatrix Potter and others bought land for the National Trust to limit development. Now, the National Trust protects 580,000 acres (232,000 hectares) of countryside in England, Wales, and Northern Ireland. It preserves over two hundred historic houses and over one hundred gardens.

Beatrix's farmhouse is now a popular tourist attraction.

More Women in Profile

There are thousands of women writers around the world. The following pages list a few more you might want to learn about on your own. The Suggested Reading list will give you further information about these women, as well as on other women writers.

1892–1973
Pearl S. Buck
The Good Earth

Pearl was raised in China, the daughter of American **missionaries**. Many of her more than eighty novels are set in China. She received a Pulitzer Prize in 1932 for *The Good Earth*. In 1938, she was the first American woman to receive the Nobel Prize in literature. More of her books have been translated than any other American author. Pearl promoted understanding among people of different cultures and races.

1890–1976
Agatha Christie
The Mousetrap

In 1920, Agatha's sister dared her to write a detective story. Agatha accepted the challenge and wrote *The Mysterious Affair at Styles*. The story began her career as one of the most popular mystery writers of all time. Agatha's books have sold over 400 million copies and have been translated into 103 languages. Her play *The Mousetrap* is the longest running play in theatrical history.

1916–
Beverly Cleary
Ramona the Pest

Beverly did not like reading when she was a child. She was bored by most stories and books. "Why couldn't authors write about the sort of boys and girls who lived on my block? ... Why couldn't they make the stories funny?" Over her almost fifty-year career as a writer and librarian, Beverly has written dozens of humorous books for young people.

Beverly Cleary

1937–

Anita Desai

The Village by the Sea

Born in India, Anita learned English when she went to school. She loved to read and, as a child, wrote and illustrated stories. Today, she writes fiction in English about characters living in India who try to balance tradition and modern life. She has taught writing at several colleges and universities in the United States.

1928–1974

Louise Fitzhugh

Harriet the Spy

Louise began her career as a painter. Many adults did not like her first novel, *Harriet the Spy*, because it showed life the way kids saw it. Young people loved it. Louise's books made it easier for authors such as Judy Blume to be published. Louise died suddenly when she was forty-six. She wrote four novels for young people and one picture book.

1950–

S.E. Hinton

The Outsiders

Susan started writing her first novel, *The Outsiders*, when she was fifteen. The book was published two years later to good reviews. Four of Susan's books have been made into films. Susan has written screenplays for her own books and has worked in the film industry.

S.E. Hinton

1918–

Madeleine L'Engle

A Wrinkle in Time

Madeleine waited for ten years before a publisher accepted her first novel, *A Wrinkle in Time*. Publishers could not decide whether the book was for children or adults. Madeleine does not label herself as a children's writer. "I just write. If the book is particularly complicated, then, of course, children are going to enjoy it more than adults."

1955–

Ann M. Martin

Baby-Sitters Club

Ann is a busy author. She writes two books a month for the popular *Baby-Sitters Club* series that has sold millions of copies. Ann is also active in her community. She supports the Ann M. Martin Foundation that funds community education and **literacy** programs for children. Ann also finds publishers to donate books to a community library program in shelters for homeless people.

Ann M. Martin

1938–

Nicholasa Mohr

El Bronx Remembered

"As a Puerto Rican child growing up in New York City, I felt invisible. I never saw myself in books. I never read a book where there were any Puerto Rican children."

Storytelling was a very important part of Nicholasa's childhood. A successful painter, she started writing stories when she was in her late thirties. Recently, she published her memoirs, *In My Own Words: Growing up inside the Sanctuary of My Imagination.*

1943–

Beverley Naidoo

Journey to Jo'burg

Beverley grew up in a white home in South Africa. As a child, she never questioned the fact that black South Africans were discriminated against and unfairly treated. As a university student, Beverley discovered how South African books for children made **racial prejudice** look acceptable. She recalls, "I still feel intensely angry about the racist deceptions ... which the adult society passed on to me as a child." She wrote her first novel for young people to show the reality of South African life. When *Journey to Jo'burg* was published in 1984, it was banned in South Africa.

1929–

Lynne Reid Banks

The Indian in the Cupboard

"My attitude toward writing is very mixed. I regard it as the hardest, loneliest work in the world, and ... I get no satisfaction until it is done."

Author of *The Indian in the Cupboard*, Lynne started her career as a stage actor and then became a television journalist. She was the first female British news reporter on television. For several years, she lived on a kibbutz, a communal farm in Israel. When she returned to England, she started to write books for young readers.

Lynne Reid Banks

1867–1957

Laura Ingalls Wilder

Little House on the Prairie

Laura often told her young daughter, Rose, stories about growing up in the pioneer days. As an adult, Rose asked her mother to write down the stories she loved as a child. Laura had already written many articles about pioneer farming life for newspapers in her home state of Missouri. When she was in her sixties, she started to write the *Little House* stories.

1927–

Maia Wojciechowska

Shadow of a Bull

Maia was twelve when World War II began. When the Nazis invaded her Polish homeland, she and her family escaped to France. Maia's book, *Till the Break of Day: Memories, 1939-1942*, tells the story of these years. Maia began writing for young people in the 1950s. In 1965, her book *Shadow of a Bull* won the Newbery Medal, an award for excellent children's literature.

1921–

Patricia Wrightson

The Crooked Snake

When she was growing up in Australia, Patricia never read books about her landscape or people. As an adult, Patricia worked to fill this gap. She is well known for using ancient Australian myths and legends in her stories. Patricia has become one of Australia's most popular writers for young people.

Glossary

abolish: to do away with a law, institution, or custom

ancestor: a relative from past generations

autobiography: a story that is written by a person about his or her own life

bigotry: when a person sticks to an opinion without considering any other ideas

civil rights: the rights of a member of a country

controversial: causing a public argument or debate

editor: someone who gets a book, magazine, or newspaper ready for publication

feminism: the belief that women should have equal rights to men

fungi: plantlike organisms that lack leaves and roots, such as mushrooms

hypocrisy: believing in one way but acting in another

literacy: being able to read and write

inauguration: the ceremony bringing a person into public office

manuscript: a book or paper that is written but not yet published

missionary: a person who goes to another country to preach religion or bring medical help

Presbyterian: a branch of the Christian religion

puberty: the stage at which a young person begins to become an adult

racial prejudice: to have an unfair opinion of people because of their race or color

segregation: to separate people

sentimental: having or showing much tender feeling

sequel: a continuation

sibling: a brother or sister

Suggested Reading

Bauermeister, Erica et al. *500 Great Books by Women: A Reader's Guide*. New York: Penguin, 1994.

Buchan, Elizabeth. *Beatrix Potter*. London: Hamish Hamilton, 1987.

Gillen, Mollie. *Lucy Maud Montgomery*. Don Mills, Ontario: Fitzhenry & Whiteside, 1978.

Greenwood, Barbara and Audrey McKim. *Her Special Vision: A Biography of Jean Little*. Toronto: Irwin Publishing, 1987.

Hurwitz, Johanna. *Astrid Lindgren: Storyteller to the World*. New York: Viking Kestrel, 1989.

Kovacs, Deborah. *Meet the Authors: 25 Writers of Upper Elementary and Middle School Books Talk About Their Work*. New York: Scholastic, 1995.

Kovacs, Deborah and James Preller. *Meet the Authors and Illustrators*. New York: Scholastic, 1993.

Lee, Betsy. *Judy Blume's Story*. Minneapolis: Dillon Press, 1981.

Magill, Frank, ed. *Great Women Writers: The Lives and Works of 135 of the World's Most Important Women Writers, from Antiquity to the Present*. New York: Holt, 1994.

Shapiro, Miles. *Maya Angelou*. New York: Chelsea House Publishers, 1994.

Index

1 2 3 4 5 6 7 8 9 0 Printed in Canada 7 6 5 4 3 2 1 0 9 8